# Suck it Up

## and
## Step Out

# Suck it Up

## and
## Step Out

It's not the things you wish for or
whine about that come about.

It's the things you passionately want
in life that make all the difference.

*by*
## Dr. L. Scot Knight

THINK PUBLISHING COMPANY
Round Rock, Texas

# Suck It Up and Step Out

Published specifically for the Direct Selling Industry by
Dream House Publishing, P.O. Box 2650, Broken Arrow, OK 74013

Unless otherwise indicated all Scripture quotations are taken
from the *King James Version* of the Bible.

Cover design by Jeff Daigle

Printed in the United States of America.

ISBN 192949614-1

# This book is dedicated to three very special women in my life:

My mama, Sharon, my friend who made so many sacrifices on my behalf regardless of all the struggles and outcome; who has always been my number one fan. Believing in me, she helped make me the person I am today.

My beautiful wife, Tara, my soul mate who has believed in me from the very beginning; who has taken me for who I am and has always supported me in everything I do. Her positive outlook on life continues to encourage and amaze me.

My daughter, Paleigh, who has taught me that the best things in life are simple—that a smile and a hug can make all the difference!

# Table of Contents

# Acknowledgments

I'm learning that it takes many people to make a book happen and God brought me some of the best.

I thank God that he allowed me to contact author, Norma Jean Lutz, to help pull these stories out of me and put them in a proper order.

Thanks to Juanelle Teague, my speaking coach and consultant, who gave me great encouragement and direction and helped me to stay focused. My acting coach Janice Dean who helped to bring out the *real* Scot, teaching me to be *me!* My close friend, Dr. Shayne Walker, who always has the right words at the right time, and is always there for me in the time of need.

Thanks also to other family members and friends who have been a positive influence in my life. I appreciate all of you.

I thank my Lord Jesus Christ to Whom I give all the praise and glory. I would never be where I am today without His love, guidance, and enabling power.

66

*You can BE,*

*you can DO,*

*and you can HAVE anything*

*in life you WANT —*

*if you want it badly enough!*

**Suck it up and step out!**

**– Scot Knight's Mama**

99

# Chapter 1
# Remembering What Mama Said

I sat in my car in the parking lot behind my chiropractic clinic, staring at the back door. Hot tears burned in my eyes turning the scene fuzzy and gray. Depression held such a grip on me, I was frozen in place. How would I ever be able to get through another day?

No one in chiropractic school ever warned me it would be this hard. In fact, no one had told me how to run a business at all. Only two months earlier, I'd moved to this small Oklahoma town to start my practice. After selecting a prime location for the clinic (which had miraculously been set up as a doctor's office), my wife, Tara, my mother, and I painted every room. We found remnant carpeting for a bargain and had it installed, then purchased a few decorative items such as pictures for the walls. It all looked so fresh and clean and promising.

With great anticipation we scheduled our grand opening, May 9, 1994. That special day brought scores of people into the clinic—the Chamber of Commerce, reporters from the local newspaper, neighboring business owners, and even a few of our family members. We received plants, floral arrangements, and congratulatory cards. A few days later it was as though we'd held a funeral instead of a grand opening.

I felt like a miserable failure. What had gone wrong? I'd spent eight years in school and even though I wasn't the best student in the world, I'd made it through. I now had the right to put the name *doctor* in front of my name. I'd paid to put all the right advertisements in the local paper. But day after day, I drove up to the clinic and maybe had one appointment on the books, on a good day, two or three.

I had no family in the town where we'd moved from my native Texas. At that time, I'd never even heard of call forwarding. I didn't own a cell phone. I couldn't afford to hire an assistant. I was the receptionist, the office manager, the doctor and the janitor. And it felt like a jail cell!

Originally, I had attempted to get the proper financing to open my practice, but no bank would talk to me. And who could blame them? I hadn't worked in four years, and I had $115,000 in college debts dogging my heels.

I was fortunate that one of my kindly kinfolk agreed to loan me $10,000 to get started. When some of my classmates from chiropractic school heard that I was planning to open a clinic with only $10,000, they tried not to laugh, but they let me know they thought I was out of my mind. Some of them were getting loans for $30 and $40 thousand and they were convinced no one could get started on only ten. There were moments when I seriously wondered if they had been right.

A local banker had fronted me $2,000 which helped some. But after paying off a knee-deep stack of bills, I had a measly $250 left to my name. I was behind in my car payments, the rent was due, and I faced yet another boring, dead day confined inside my clinic. The twin monsters of boredom and depression had me hammered down flat. I lay my head on the steering wheel of my car and just sat there overcome with feelings of hopelessness and helplessness. I saw no way I could make it.

I couldn't tell you how or what I prayed as I sat there that morning alone in my car, but I know it was a cry of desperation. I'm not even sure how I found the strength to get out of my car, unlock that clinic door and go inside. But I did. And just as sure as I did, God was busy answering my prayer.

## Mama's Words

Somewhere in the course of that morning, I began to remember the words my Mama had spoken to me all through my growing up years.

It first began when she and my father were divorced. She sat me down and said, "Scot, there are going to be times in life when things don't seem fair, and when life may not go right. BUT...

*You can BE, you can DO, you can HAVE anything*
*in life you WANT—if you want it badly enough.*

Those words had already brought me through a number of adversities in my life. And that wasn't all my Mama taught me. She also told me that there may be times when things may not go my way. I might have to tighten my belt a few notches. But when that happened, Mama said,

"Just... ***Suck it up and step out!***"

If ever there had been a time to take Mama at her word that time was now—in that lonely clinic where hundreds of patients were *not* breaking down my doors to come in and be treated. What did I truly *want*? What did I passionately *want*? What did I *want* with every fiber of my being?

I wanted to have a successful chiropractic clinic in this little town in the Midwest where my only competition was *one other chiropractor.* I realized the choice was mine. I could sit around and continue to whine and cry. Or I could

***Suck it up and step out!***

Thankfully, I chose the latter.

It finally dawned on me that if people were not coming to me, then I would have to go to them. I started locking up the clinic for an hour every day. For that hour I walked up and down Main Street to visit my business neighbors. I smiled real big and

I shook hands with a firm, confident handshake. "Hi," I said, "my name is Scot, Scot Knight." (I never said "doctor." What did they care whether or not I was a doctor?) "I'm the new chiropractor in town. I've been in practice about two months. I want to give you my card." After making sure the card was firmly in that person's hand, I said, "If you know of anyone who could use chiropractic care, or if I can help you or your family out, I'd greatly appreciate the business."

Up and down the streets I went. I shook hands, I chatted, I smiled, I asked about their kids and their businesses. My new motto was this: "The more people I meet and greet, the more people I treat!"

I ordered a big box of ballpoint pens with my clinic name and phone number printed on them. I walked into Wal-Mart with a fist full of pens and handed them out to everyone. I had 5,000 brightly-colored flyers printed with information about my clinic and hired junior-high kids to take them door-to-door. My wife and I attended every community event we could, from ball games to the Chamber of Commerce functions to the local Rotary club meetings. I got to know people; people got to know me. A few began to trust me and come for treatment. They, in turn, told their friends.

The turn-around did not happen overnight. The bottom line is: the turn-around *did happen*! But it never would have

- if I had not known my WANT
- if I had not *wanted* it passionately
- if I had not instigated a workable plan
- if I had not put that plan into action
- if I had not *sucked it up and stepped out*

In order to help relate the full meaning of WANT, consider the following acronym:

## W You want it? You give it!

Whatever you're willing to put in and give is what you will pull out and get. There is a price to pay—a sacrifice to make. Getting what you want in life will not be the easy route to take.

Film director Sidney Howard once said, *One-half of knowing what you want, is knowing what you must give up before you get it.* The Bible calls it "counting the cost." (Luke 14:28)

Counting the cost means you must recognize the *internal drive* that fires you up and fuels your life. It means you must connect with your *hidden spark,* the craving (or desire) that ignites your internal drive!

## A Act on it!

Step out and take action, and turn your dreams into goals. (We'll talk more about how to do this later in the book.) Begin to envision your *undeniable want-to* that will set your course with a clear direction. (Your undeniable want-to is a WANT that is so strong, it cannot be denied!)

Without a vision, the Bible tells us, people perish. (Proverbs 29:18) And people do perish with no vision—we all do. Until we can *see*—visualize—our WANTs, we will never set out in a clear direction to reach them.

Write the vision and make it plain, Habakkuk 3:3 tells us, so those who read it may *run.* Envisioning and writing out the vision speeds up the process. This is the point where you decide where *you* want to go in life and what *you* want to do.

## N Navigate it!

Create a clear plan of action and follow it by writing goals and assigning deadlines to them. I call this a *time-bound strategy* which will serve to keep you right on course. What will it take to achieve your goals and how soon can you get there? That's what navigating is all about. People who aim at nothing often hit it. To be directionless is extremely unsettling! People who are directionless stumble over the least little obstacle that rears its ugly head.

## T Taste it!

Keep your "eye on the prize" and taste the sweetness of victory before it ever comes! By visualizing your final focus—your final destination—you will be better prepared to overcome any difficulties or obstacles that arise in your path.

## What Are *Your* WANTs?

All four stages of WANT are important and each one will be explained further as the book progresses.

## The Rest of the Story

Four short years after that fateful day sitting out behind my clinic, I sold that $10,000 practice for an amazing $150,000 and moved—along with my beautiful wife—back to the Lone Star State a very happy man!

I sucked it up, I stepped out and I wound up a winner. Mama's words of wisdom had won out once again.

That is basically what this book is all about. My mama's words will work not only for her one and only favorite son, they will work for anyone and everyone who dares to put the concept into action.

This book is for people who lack direction in life and aren't sure how to find and identify their WANT. Within every person there lay hidden sparks. Those *sparks* are the things in life that that you truly WANT—the passions of your life.

It will be those hidden sparks that ultimately

1. connect with your internal drive

2. fire up the internal drive, and

3. keep you going forward on the right track

## Wish-y Wants

Many people today have lost their fire, their passion, their hidden sparks. The WANTs that drove them in years past are now reduced to what I call *wish-y wants*. These are weak, wishy-washy wishes, that serve as a poor excuse for passionate WANTs! *Wish-y wants* drive people to play the lottery and the sweepstakes, head to Vegas and play the "one-armed bandit" hoping and wishing for a stroke of luck. While they sit around wishing, they seem to be totally unaware that they are stuck in a long, deep rut.

What is the difference between a wish-y want and an undeniable WANT? That difference is *YOU*.

### Wish – Y want
### o
### u

*You* are the deciding factor in the matter.

But for many people, their hidden sparks have been doused by floods of adverse circumstances—or by the harsh words of negative people. As a result, their internal drive has been altered, injured, or impaired.

While it's not my intention to belittle or diminish anyone's pain, misfortune or heartbreak, ultimately the choices in life are still up to *you*. Do you give up? Or do you suck it up?

The stories and examples included in this book are designed to encourage you to go back and rekindle your hidden sparks. To put the whining, crying and pity parties aside, and to *suck it up and step out*!

## Suck-It-Up Summary

- You can BE, you can DO, you can HAVE anything in life you WANT—if you want it badly enough

- Suck it up and step out!

- Remember the WANT acronym: Want it? Give it; Act on it; Navigate it; Taste it

- Recognize, identify wish-y wants; trade them in for undeniable WANTs

## Suck-It-Up Steps to Success

Make a list of your dreams that you have allowed to become wish-y wants. Only YOU can turn them into viable goals.

_____

_____

_____

_____

_____

_____

_____

_____

Make a list of the WANTs in your life. What are the dreams and desires that you have placed on the back burner for whatever reason—or *reasons*.

_____

_____

_____

_____

_____

_____

List the actions you will need to take to reach your desired goals.

_____

_____

_____

_____

_____

_____

66

*It's not the things in life*
*you wish for and whine about*
*that come about.*
*It's the things you passionately WANT*
*that make all the difference.*

**– Scot Knight**

99

# Chapter 2
# A WANT Awakening

## Mama's Encouragement

I'm a proud Texan from the West Texas town of Monahans. I grew up under the love, care, and nurture of my mother who worked for years as a secretary to support us. She was my biggest fan and chief encourager.

Although I was never a good student (actually I hated school), my mama continually gave me positive input, never condemning. When most other kids were getting money for bringing home A's and B's on their grade cards, my mama threw a party when I brought home a C. She raved about my performance when I had made the least little bit of progress. In her eyes, I was the best and the brightest and she never let me forget it. Surely at times, I must have been a disappointment to her. Surely at times, she must have been discouraged when she saw how low my grades were, but she never once let on. Her attitude was never anything but *up*.

In high school all I had on my mind was sports, parties and girls—not necessarily in that order. As I approached the end of my senior year, I began to have second thoughts about college. I saw how my mother had struggled all her life to try and support me and realized I wanted more from my own life. Of course, Mama had been encouraging me all along to study harder and strive to go to college, but it fell on deaf ears. Now suddenly I had a change of heart. I started checking into what it would take to attend college.

## A WANT Is Born

The first step, I learned, was to take the ACT test. I did this three months before graduation. What a rude awakening that turned out to be. Only two people in my life know how low that score actually was—my mama and my wife! I was humiliated, but I was not defeated.

Angelo State University in San Angelo, Texas, the university I applied to, said in essence that I simply was not college material. Their kindest suggestion was that I attend a junior college for a year and then *maybe* apply with the university the following spring. That was not an acceptable plan in my mind, because I had found a hidden spark that was firing up my internal drive. A WANT was being born. I wanted to attend college that fall and nothing less was acceptable to me at the moment.

This was the first time in my life that I had the awakening of a genuine WANT. Oh sure, I'd had wants before (and I'll tell about those later in the book) but I wasn't totally responsible for the outcome of those wants. With this situation, it all depended on me. What were my options?

In order to get what we WANT in life we have to give what it takes to get it. I saw I was going to have to do two things: I needed to get a job to earn money for tuition, and I needed to enroll in some college courses. This called for a clear plan of action.

## Step Out and Take Action

I landed a job in the West Texas oil fields as a roustabout, and I enrolled in night summer school at Odessa Junior College. That meant during the summer following my graduation, while all my buddies were at the swimming pool, going on dates, and taking family vacations, I got up every morning at six. I grabbed up the big old lunch my mama packed for me and drove 45 minutes to the oil fields. I worked all day digging holes under the broiling

West Texas sun, wearing a hard hat and steel-toed boots. When the workday was over, I drove home gobbled down a sandwich, then drove 45 minutes the opposite direction to Odessa. I attended class from 6:30 to 10:00, after which I drove back home, went to bed, got up the next morning and did it all over again.

I've already stated that I was not a good student, but I did memorize easily. I learned to make notes and put them in my pockets. Out in the oil fields I would pull out my notes and study as I worked.

By the end of the summer I had thirteen hours of college credit and had earned enough money to pay for my tuition for my freshman year at school. And most exciting of all, I was accepted into Angelo State University in the fall just as I had planned.

Mama's words never rang truer than at that moment in my life:

*You can BE, you can DO, you can HAVE anything*
*in life you WANT—if you want it badly enough.*

These were no longer just words to me; they had become a way of life. I had lived out the four steps for having the things in life I wanted.

## W You want it? You give it?

I was willing to give up a summer of fun and games in order to earn money for college that fall.

## A Act on it!

I was willing to take whatever actions were required of me.

## N Navigate it! Create a clear plan of action and follow it

I laid out a course of action and followed it faithfully day after day.

**T** Taste it! Keep your "eye on the prize" and taste the sweetness of victory!

When weariness set in and when I was ready to give up, I encouraged myself by remembering the prize—to be accepted by the college of my choice in the fall.

I had discovered the hidden sparks which fired me up, and connected with my inner drive that propelled me down the path toward my goal. This new revelation was still very under-developed at this time. I was not yet creating time-bound strategies in my life, and I wasn't seasoned enough to harness the power of the four stages of WANT. It was, however, a clear step in the right direction. I could have easily had a pity party. I could have accepted defeat. But I sucked it up and I stepped out. And it paid off in big dividends.

## The "No-Leg" Pilot

In December, 1931, a young British pilot named Doug Bader nearly lost his life in a plane crash that pulverized his plane. To save his life, doctors were forced to amputate his right leg above the knee and the left leg six inches below the knee.

As he lay in the hospital following the accident, an undeniable WANT arose in Bader's heart and mind. He was determined to fly again.

For months he struggled to learn to walk on artificial legs and when he was mobile, he applied to the Royal Air Force for a return to flight duty, but was turned down. However, when England went to war with Germany in 1939, trained pilots were in short supply. Soon Bader was back in the military in the midst of the Battle of Britain.

Within the span of one short year, Bader shot down 22 German planes. Eventually he was given command of a 60-plane unit. Separated from his squadron over occupied-France in 1941, Bader was shot down and captured by the Germans.

The Germans so admired his courage they allowed the RAF to parachute in a new artificial leg to replace the one Bader lost when he was shot down. When he was again mobile, Bader attempted escape so many times he was finally locked in the formidable castle known as Colditz prison until his liberation at the end of the war.

Bader's story is a perfect example of the awakening of an undeniable WANT, the fulfillment of that WANT, and the action required to achieve desired results!

## Suck-It-Up Summary

- an undeniable WANT requires recognition
- an undeniable WANT requires action

## Suck-It-Up Steps to Success

In a short paragraph describe one or two of your undeniable wants and how it might be awakened:

_____

_____

_____

_____

_____

_____

_____

"

*In any situation, ask yourself:*
*What strengths do I possess that*
*can contribute towards accomplishing*
*something in this situation?*
*Then follow through.*

• • • • •

*It is your hidden sparks*
*that will ignite your internal drive.*

**– Scot Knight**

"

# Chapter 3
# Finding Your Hidden Sparks

## Some Sparks Ignite Slowly

Some dreams evolve slowly over time. They need time to formulate and mature. For instance, the seed of the WANT to become a chiropractor came about for me first of all when I was still in high school.

I had hurt my lower back while running in track. I went to the team doctor, the trainer, and the medical doctors, but all they could offer was pain medication. It helped some, but I didn't want the pain to be killed, I wanted to be able to run track again. Finally, I went to the chiropractor down the street. After two adjustments the pain was completely gone and I was back to running again, good as new.

At that moment it crossed my mind that I would like to be a chiropractor myself one day, because I enjoyed helping people. But as quickly as that thought came, another thought followed just as quickly: "I may want to be a chiropractor, but I never could. I'm just not smart enough. Too much science for me to handle. After all," I reminded myself, "I *am* a D student. Not exactly the best candidate."

And that was that. For the time being the matter was closed, but a tiny spark had been ignited.

Years later, when I was a senior at Angelo State University, I dated a cheerleader who had gone to chiropractors all her life. She had injured her neck, and she asked me to go with her to the chiropractic clinic for her appointments, and I agreed.

This chiropractor was young, energetic, and fun. I could tell immediately that he loved what he did. Now the little spark inside me flared up again. I was thinking, "I like this guy. I could do this and really enjoy it."

The problem, however, was this. As I struggled directionless through college, I'd already changed my major *five* times, finally settling on psychology. (I had definitely chosen a career where I could help people.) How could I just stop that course of action, change completely, and go to chiropractic school? People would sure enough think I'd gone bonkers. I wasn't sure I could bear up under those negative reactions.

As I was struggling with all those conflicting thoughts, I learned that one of the senior guys in the dorm room next to me was planning to go to chiropractic school after his graduation. He gave me all the brochures and information I needed—I didn't even have to seek out the materials myself. It seemed like a real confirmation to me, so I began to pray about the matter.

When I talked to Mama about it, she said just what she'd always said to me. "Scot, you can do anything you put your mind to do. If this is what you really want, then do it!"

Before I graduated from Angelo State, that hidden spark was raging and had ignited my internal drive. All of a sudden it didn't matter that I'd just completed four years in college majoring in psychology. It didn't matter that I didn't really like school, or like to study. I was ready to go! I had moved from a *wish-y want* to a genuine WANT! This WANT was so strong, I was driven to action. I even attempted to sell my car that I'd purchased only a month earlier, and made plans to move to Dallas.

Even though this spark was slow to come about, once it was fanned and had ignited my inner drive I was ready and willing to suck it up and step out.

## Finding Your Hidden Sparks

What are your hidden sparks? What are those things in life that you really and truly want? What are your passions? Your dreams? Your goals?

Is it to

- spend more quality time with your family?
- go back to school and get that degree?
- take a long-overdue vacation?
- set up a personal fitness program?
- start your own business?

Take time to think about and consider your internal drive. Every person has an internal drive, but every person's is different. The same thing that fires me up may leave you bored stiff. And what drives you to action may not interest me in the least.

What excites you? What pushes you forward? What fires you up deep inside? What makes you say yes when all circumstances are saying no? What makes you eager to jump out of bed every single morning—to face the new day with energy and excitement?

Once you can answer those questions, you will know and understand your own internal drive. You will understand what motivates you. And once you understand what motivates you, you are then better equipped to cooperate with your own personal internal drive.

Determining what you truly WANT, and doing whatever it takes, morally and ethically, to get there will change your life. You will move out of the doldrums and leap ahead into overdrive with more than enough energy to succeed.

## Bantam Ben

In the 1920s a little boy in Fort Worth, Texas, found he could earn money to help his widowed mother by caddying on the golf course. Small for his age and extremely quiet, he became the perfect caddy, prompting the better players to ask for him at the course. Quietly, the boy studied all the moves, learning the course and the game *in his mind*. The more he watched, the more his hidden spark was ignited and his WANT was awakened. He knew he wanted to be able to play golf.

Ben was a teenager before he could save enough money to purchase a set of used clubs. The problem was, the clubs were right-handed and he was a lefty. Or at least it *seemed* like a problem. But not for this young man. He simply made up his mind to think and function right-handed. Ben sucked it up and stepped out.

While the other caddies rested between games, the little Bantam, as he came to be called, practiced relentlessly. At first, his pint size limited his strength in his drive, but that too he worked hard to overcome by developing his own personal style. His strongest asset, he quickly discovered, was his ability to concentrate on his game in spite of any and all distractions on the course.

By the mid 1930s Ben was playing on the PGA, and after seven long dry years, he finally emerged as one of the winners. Ben Hogan soon became a force to contend with and went on to become one of our country's most beloved professional golfers. But it all began when as a little boy, his WANT awakened within him and he followed it through in spite of obstacles.

## Suck-It-Up Summary

- find your own personal hidden sparks which will in turn ignite your internal drive
- learn what motivates you; what fires you up
- realize hidden sparks may not emerge overnight; be patient

## Suck-It-Up Steps to Success

Make a list of the deep hidden sparks in your life. What is it specifically that motivates you?

_____

_____

_____

_____

_____

_____

_____

**"**

*Every action has an equal
and opposite criticism.*

• • • • •

*The problem is not the problem.
The problem is one's attitude
about the problem.*

**"**

# Chapter 4
# Never Take "No" for an Answer

## Friday Night Football

When you grow up in a West Texas town like Monahans, you learn very early the seriousness of Friday night football. Friday night football is more than just a sport, it's a community tradition and a way of life. The whole town turns out for the games. The whole town drives to the away games. From my earliest memories of school, my dream was to put on the green and white and be a Monahans Lobo. That dream came close to being dashed, however, and that's when I learned a big lesson in not taking "no" for an answer.

To explain fully, I have to go back to a moment in time when I was only eight years old—a time when my mother had decided that she and I would move into a second floor apartment.

## A Near-Fatal Fall

As a little kid, I became bored easily. I was always looking for something to do and therefore often got into mischief. While Mama was unpacking boxes and putting things away, there was nothing for me to do. I asked her for permission to go outside. I told her I was going to see if I could meet some new friends.

I went outside, but instead of going downstairs to look for friends, I became fascinated with the balcony railing on the outside stairs. As I looked at it, I could see that I could lie down in the space between the guardrail in the lower part, and the handrail on top. In experimental fashion I fit my body into that space lying on my back and holding onto the handrail to keep my balance. Looking over to my left there was the apartment balcony. As I looked to my right, there was only concrete—two stories down.

This was pretty neat. It was a daring feat for an eight-year-old. But it wasn't enough. I knew I could do more. I wondered if I could let go of the handrail, clap my hands once and grab hold again. It was a good plan, but it failed. The next thing I knew I fell two stories down hitting the concrete with full impact on my back. I lay there unable to breathe because the wind was knocked out of me.

It seemed an eternity before I could take even a short breath, and when I did the pain was deep and severe. I could barely crawl back up the stairs. As soon as I opened the apartment door, I saw my mama. She said, "Well hi, Sugar. Did you have fun?"

"Yes ma'am," I said. I wasn't about to tell her what happened. I'd already lost my breath once.

So Mama continued to unpack boxes and I decided to lie down on the couch and began to doze off.

## God's Angel

Shortly, there came a knock at our door. My mother opened the door and there stood a tall, dark-haired man. "I'm your neighbor from downstairs," he explained, "and if I'm not mistaken, I could swear I just saw your son fly past my window."

Now Mama was pretty shocked by this announcement. She turned around to me. "Scot? Are you all right?" I stood up to prove to her that I was. "I'm okay, Mama." Then I lay back down—quickly.

We convinced our neighbor that everything was all right so he left. I'm not sure if he made it to the bottom step, because in a few short moments he was knocking at the door again. "Ma'am," he said, "I don't want to keep bothering you but that boy fell and he fell hard. I think we ought to go get him checked out."

"What do you mean?" Mama asked.

"I think we ought to take him to the hospital just to be sure."

Mama was finally convinced. She drove her car, the neighbor man rode along with us, and I was lying down in the back seat. I remember insisting that I was all right and that I didn't need to go to the hospital. I was hoping I could talk Mama out of this, because I didn't want to see a doctor.

At the Monahans hospital they took my vital signs only to learn that I had no blood pressure which meant I was bleeding internally. Within half an hour of arriving at the hospital, I was transferred by ambulance to Odessa Children's Hospital for emergency surgery.

At first they thought it was my liver, but instead it was my right kidney which had been ruptured by the fall. It was quickly removed and I was placed in the Intensive Care for three days.

I must interject here that looking back on the accident and the favorable outcome, I truly believe that my downstairs neighbor, Mr. Denver Blue, was an angel sent from God to save my life. I never think about it without thanking God for taking care of me. A few more hours and I surely would have died.

## The Promise

Now back to the subject of Friday night football. While I was in the ICU I received a special letter of encouragement from the coaches of Monahans High School football team. It read:

*Dear Scot:*

*We hope you are feeling much better by now. Do what the doctor says: if you do, you will be healthy and strong. One of these days we look forward to your putting on a Lobo uniform and playing for the Mean Green.*

*Take care of yourself. We are going to win the game for you against Fort Stockton this Friday night.*

This letter was signed by John T. Ratcliff, Assistant Principal, the 1975 Varsity Football Team, and all the Varsity coaches. Pretty heady stuff for an eight-year-old to receive. That Friday night game was dedicated to me—a little boy lying in a hospital room recuperating from surgery. That was the most special letter I'd ever received in my young life—but it would become even more special in years to come.

## Never Accept "No"

When I entered into Junior High, I was playing football, happily moving toward my dream. But when it came time for me to go out for the varsity team, we were required to take a physical. A doctor came to the school and one by one he gave each player a physical. On the exam sheet he would write, "approved" or "failed." After my physical, my sheet had a "failed" written on it.

"I'm sorry," the doctor told me, "but we cannot allow you to play football with only one kidney. The liability would be too great."

Not play football? After having played since seventh grade? After nurturing this dream all these years? Not be allowed to suit up with the varsity squad? I couldn't believe this turn of events. The word *devastation* doesn't even begin to describe what I felt at that moment.

Everything changed, however, as soon as Mama heard what had happened. Mama got on the phone and called the head trainer and demanded to know what was going on. The trainer told her as politely as he could about the liability of my playing high school football. But Mama just said to him, "My son WILL play football."

Now my mama could have said to me, "You know Scot, let's stop and think about this. They do have a point. Perhaps it *would* be dangerous for you to play high school football." But she never said that. She saw how much it meant to me. She knew it had been my dream all my growing up years. So Mama went straight to her filing cabinet and started searching through the file folders. And what did she pull out of the drawer? The letter written to me by the coaches of Monahans High School when I was eight years old. And guess who was now the superintendent of the school? One of the coaches who had signed the letter nine years earlier, Head Coach Jerry Larned.

Mama took the letter to the school, went directly to his office, and placed the letter in front of him. Reminding him of the promise he had made to a little eight-year-old boy, she said, "Now, Mr. Larned, you tell him he can't play football?"

A week later, I was putting on the green-and-white and calling myself a Monahans Lobo and playing Friday night football. The school even paid for my $500 kidney pad that I wore for every game.

Mama taught me a valuable lesson in that situation—never accept the word "No." If you believe in it, if you want it, if you know it's right, never *never* accept the word NO.

## Jean Driscoll Refuses the "No's"

Jean Driscoll faced an uphill battle as a child born in 1966 with spina bifida, leaving her unable to walk properly. In spite of leg braces and dragging feet, she was determined to be like the other kids. By sheer grit she learned to ride a friend's ten-speed bicycle.

Her condition, however, worsened and by the time she was a teenager she was confined to a wheel chair. Her spirits plummeted and by age nineteen she turned suicidal because she felt her life was a total waste.

It was the discovery of wheelchair sports that changed Jean's life. University of Illinois wheelchair coach Brad Hedrick recruited Jean to attend his university and play for their basketball team. Suddenly, all the "no's" of her life were turned around to one resounding "go for it!" Basketball and soccer fascinated her, but it was wheelchair racing that became the hidden spark that ignited her internal drive.

Jean went on to become the only eight-time champion of the Boston Marathon in its 100+ year history. She is the only person to ever break the course and world record at the Boston Marathon five times. She was named #25 of the top 100 female athletes of the 20th century by *Sports Illustrated for Wome*n.

Jean has made multiple television appearances, was the subject of a PBS documentary, and has had numerous magazine articles featuring her life story. Streets have been named in her honor and honorary degrees have been presented to her. She's become a legend in her time, and has become an inspiration to millions.

As a little girl, Jean was told she'd only be able to make a living "sitting down and using her hands." What an interesting twist of irony that she does indeed sit down in her wheelchair during her high speed races. And she does use her hands to stroke those wheels—thousands of times in a single race with a force equal to thousands of pushups.

In the midst of all her physical training, Jean also managed to complete her undergraduate and master's degrees.

Jean Discoll sucked it up and stepped out. She would not take "no" for an answer.

You don't have to take "no" for an answer either! It's your choice.

## "They Don't Allow That"

After I'd been in my Oklahoma clinic for about a year or so, I heard about the Texas Rangers AAA baseball team in Oklahoma City, which was not far from where we were living. One day the thought came to me how great it would be to be their team chiropractor. I mentioned this to a few acquaintances and the response was, "Oh no, you can't be their team chiropractor. They don't allow that."

While I didn't agree with the negative reactions, still and yet, I had no connections and had no way to move forward on the idea. However, there are times when, if you are willing and ready, God will move the circumstances right into your midst.

One night my wife, Tara, and I were at a party and one of the catchers from the Oklahoma City ball club was there. Somehow he learned that I was a chiropractor. He came right up to me and said, "You're a chiropractor?" I said, "Yes I am." Motioning to his back he said, "Man, would you give me an adjustment? I'm in pain."

I adjusted him right there on the couch in the host's living room. But I wasn't going to let him get away easily. Before I was finished, I said, "I'd like to help your team by adjusting some of the other players. How would I go about doing that?" He gladly gave me the name and number of their team trainer.

When I called the trainer and talked to him, he was very skeptical. "Naw," he said, "we don't need anything like that. And besides you'd have to call our team orthopedic surgeon and get his permission." A little reluctantly, he gave me the surgeon's name and phone number. I thanked him and hung up.

Now here I was, a chiropractor who'd just been out of school about a year, and I have to call and talk to a skilled orthopedic surgeon. At that time, such a thing was way out of this boy's comfort zone. What should I do? I did what Mama always said do—I sucked it up and stepped out.

As quickly as my fingers could punch buttons, I had that surgeon on the phone line. "Yes sir," I said, "My name is Dr. Scot Knight and I'm a chiropractor and I'd very much like to be the team chiropractor for the Oklahoma City ball club. The team trainer said I would have to have it cleared through you first."

The surgeon was as courteous as could be. He said he had no objections at all to my being the team chiropractor, and if it was all right with the team trainer then it was certainly all right with him.

I hung up and called the team trainer back. When I told him it had been cleared by the team orthopedic surgeon, his tone changed. "That's fine," he said, "we'll call you when we need you."

Two weeks later he called. A player who'd been with the Toronto Blue Jays had been traded to the Texas Rangers AAA team and he was my first superstar athlete patient. I drove to the clubhouse and treated the superstar. I adjusted his neck and got him all aligned again, and that night he hit a home run! Of course I was thrilled. Lucky for me that baseball players are superstitious—guess how many team members wanted an adjustment that next week? Before the next game I had adjusted fifteen players.

I went on to serve as the team chiropractor for four years! It was fun, fulfilling and rewarding. I also treated players from the other teams, the managers, the coaches and a few of the umpires.

## Nothing Is Wasted

Later when I was once again living in Texas, I attended a Rotary Club meeting. Sitting at my table was Reid Ryan, son of Hall-of-Famer, baseball legend, Nolan Ryan. I had heard that the father and son were thinking about bringing a ball team to the area where I was living. So when I realized who was sitting at the same table with me, I introduced myself.

"My name is Scot Knight," I said, shaking Reid's hand, "and I was the team chiropractor with the Texas Rangers AAA team." I mentioned the name of the trainer with whom I had worked so closely. Reid recognized the name and nodded as I talked.

"Hey," I said, "if you get this team in here—and I'm sure you will—would it be possible for me to be the team chiropractor?"

Reid Ryan's answer to me was, "Absolutely!"

The point here is this. When I was first told, "That isn't allowed," I didn't accept "no" as the final answer. Instead I sucked it up and stepped out—stepped out of my comfort zone and took action. The rewards have been well worth that small risk.

## Suck-It-Up Summary

- people may say it can't be done
- circumstances may say it can't be done
- don't accept the "no"; but keep on trying
- look for new ways to approach a problem or dilemma
- answers and solutions are just waiting to be discovered
- don't let what others say dictate your actions or responses

## Suck-It-Up Steps

Never take a "no" at face value! List areas where, in the past, you allowed a "no" to be the final answer.

_____

_____

_____

_____

_____

What could you have done differently?

_____

_____

_____

_____

"

*The soul cannot think*

*without a picture.*

**– Aristotle**

• • • • •

*Where there is no vision*

*the people perish.*

**– Proverbs 29:18**

"

# Chapter 5
# What You SEE Is What You Get

Remember the old saying, *What you see is what you get*? This is usually interpreted to mean there are no hidden agendas or hidden motives. That everything on the surface level can be trusted. However, I view this saying in yet another way. What we SEE—or what we envision in our minds and in our imaginations, is ultimately what we get in life. Fortunately I happened to witness this phenomenon rather early in life.

## A Different Warm-up

In addition to football, I also went out for track when I was in high school. My favorite track event was the hurdles. I became a pretty fair hurdler, placing second in district and going on to the regionals. At every track meet there were different classes of schools represented: Class 1A, 2A, 3A, 4A and 5A—5A being the largest schools.

One of the best track stars at our events was a plucky black guy named Gary from Odessa Permian High School. Because Odessa was a larger school than Monahans, I did not compete against Gary and I was mighty thankful for that.

I remember one track meet when I, along with all the other guys, was out on the field stretching, warming up, joking around, and basically acting goofy like high school guys do. All of a sudden I noticed off to the side Gary, the Odessa track star, was sitting on the ground all by himself. His knees were drawn up, his head down on his knees and the hood of his jacket pulled over his head. I wondered if something was wrong, so I went over to him.

"Hey Gary," I said, "aren't you going to warm up with the rest of us?"

Peeking out from under the hood, he said, "I *am* warming up."

I thought he was kidding. "No, I'm talking about stretching and getting ready for the race."

"Right now," he said using his most patient tone of voice, "I am visualizing the race in my mind. I see myself getting in the box. I hear the gun going off. I see myself clearing the first hurdle, the second hurdle, the third hurdle, and going over the very last hurdle and crossing the finish line first! That's how I warm up for my race."

As I look back on that scene today, I know that Gary was making perfect sense. He was using the technique of visualization in order to win his game. But at the time he could have been talking Greek. I didn't understand a word of it. I shrugged and said, "Yeah, whatever." And went back to stretching, warming up, and acting goofy with my buddies. But I do remember this— Gary won every race!

That brief conversation with Gary at the track meet was my very first introduction to visualization. A small seed was planted in my mind.

## Learning How to Visualize

Years later while attending college, I worked at a private psychiatric hospital in San Angelo as a mental health technician. I worked the night shift where it was my job every fifteen minutes to check on certain people who were suicidal. It wasn't exactly a demanding job. While working there I met a psychologist named John Allison.

John's thatch of gray hair and deeply-lined face spoke of experience and wisdom and he quickly became my friend and mentor. When he spoke, his deep, raspy voice had a definite calming and settling effect—something this college boy needed. As we spent the long nights talking together, he began teaching me the basic elements of visualization.

One of John's specialties was the classes he taught on relaxation methods, and one of the techniques he stressed was that of visualization. John explained to me about the conscious and the subconscious mind.

"The subconscious mind," he told me, "is one step below the conscious mind. The subconscious mind doesn't know the difference between truth and non-truth. So whatever your subconscious mind hears and receives, it will believe. In other words," he added, "whatever *you* tell your subconscious mind, it will believe."

This was new to me, but I liked what I was hearing. That was at the very time in my life when I was considering changing my choice of profession to becoming a chiropractor and John said to me, "Do you know what you want in life?"

"Yes, sir," I said, "I want to be a chiropractor."

"Do you know how to get there?"

Always being a cutup I said, "Sure. You get on the highway and head east." Because the school I would attend was located in Dallas.

"No, no. I mean do you know how to visualize what you want in life?"

The truth was I had no idea at all how to visualize what I wanted in life. But John patiently began to teach me. I loved the concept and took to it like a duck to water. Before you know it I was visualizing everything about being a chiropractor long before I ever became one. I could see it, taste it, feel it, hear it. I saw the sign that said, *Knight Chiropractic Clinic*. I saw myself driving up to the clinic, getting out of my car and going inside. I saw myself turning on all the lights. I saw myself examining and treating my patients. The phone was ringing. I picked it up and answered, "Knight Chiropractic, this is Dr. Knight speaking, may I help you?" All of this envisioning took place before I was ever accepted into chiropractic school.

By learning how to harness my imagination and put it to work for me, I learned yet another new truth and valuable lesson in life: *What you focus upon, you ultimately move toward*. Or, as stated earlier, *What you SEE is what you get.*

## Envisioning: Olympian Thinking

I've heard many accounts of the results of envisioning and some are pretty amazing. The most amazing, however, is the account of Olympic star Marilyn King. By her own admission, Marilyn was never a great athlete, but she was a powerful competitor. That ability, she has said, had much more to do with her mind than her physical prowess.

She was a member of the U.S. Olympic team in the 1972 and 1976 games competing in the Pentathlon. The pentathlon consists of five track and field events, a grueling and demanding event. While in training for the upcoming 1980 games, Marilyn was injured in a head-on collision that left her flat on her back in bed. At a time when most people would have given up, Marilyn never even considered the option. In her mind, she determined she would not end her career in bed, or even less than fully able to again compete in the Olympics.

From her bed she spent hours watching films of pentathletes projected on the ceiling. She chose films of the world-record holders in all five of her events. In her mind's eye, she saw herself competing, mentally rehearsing every event. When she was not watching films, she visualized the events and saw herself competing in vivid detail. Once she was on her feet again, she physically walked the course, all the while envisioning herself competing and winning.

Even though Marilyn King had not spent hours in physical practice, she placed second at the 1980 Olympic trials. Because the 1980 Olympics were cancelled, no one will ever know what Marilyn might have done, but she certainly proved what envisioning can do.

Marilyn became so fascinated by mental rehearsing, or envisioning, that she went on to do extensive research into what she termed, *Olympian Thinking*. In her hometown of Oakland, California, she developed a program called Dare to Imagine helping inner city youth to discover their passions in life and then develop a map of how to follow those passions.

It was exactly what John Allison taught me and it's something I now use everyday of my life. What you *see* is truly what you get in life.

## Suck-It-Up Summary

- what you SEE is what you GET
- visualize the end result
- you will ultimately move toward that which you focus upon

## Suck-It-Up Steps to Success

Make a list of the areas in which you will begin to visualize the end result of your dream.

Make a list of ways in which you can aid the visualization, i.e. photos, pictures, film clips, watching experts at work, visiting the site or sites where such activities occur.

_____

_____

_____

_____

_____

_____

_____

_____

**"**

*Obstacles are those frightful things you see*
*when you take your mind off your goals.*

• • • • •

*Write the vision and*
*make it plain upon tables*
*that he may run that reads it.*

**– Habakkuk 2:2**

**"**

# Chapter 6
# How're You Going to Get There?

## Write the Vision; Map the Plan

B efore a pilot of any size aircraft takes off on a flight, whether it be a short hop or cross country, he never leaves without first making a detailed flight plan.

When you and your family go on vacation, chances are you sit down first and make travel arrangements and map out your course. You have flight arrangements, hotel reservations, and possibly even tickets to events or theme parks you will visit. Lists of what to pack are strewn all over the house, as are various flyers and brochures, all of which assist you in making your plans.

Think about it—even a trip to the grocery store demands that you scribble out a list. It may be scribbled on the back of an old envelope, but it's still a written plan.

When it comes to making life-plans, however, many people come up short. More time and attention is spent planning for a vacation or a trip to the grocery store, than setting goals to reach new levels and improving quality of life.

## Drifting Through Life

When I was growing up, the word "goals" to me meant the posts at each end of the football field, or the nets at each end of the basketball court. I had no concept of writing out goals and putting my plans into actions. Throughout high school I was virtually directionless. For most of my college years, I was still basically directionless. I was a drifting ship with a broken rudder and shredded sails; wherever the wind happened to blow that's the direction I drifted.

But once I discovered the passion to become a chiropractor, then I realized it was time to make and follow a clear plan of action.

In the WANT acronym, this is the "N" for navigate. Without a map, a clear plan of action, a precise strategy, you will flounder from one directionless day to the next. If there is any advancement in the right direction, it is usually accidental, and it is never measurable. Without a set of goals that are written out, how can you determine how close you are to the finish line?

When the pilot starts out on the journey, there may come turbulence or other outside circumstances which forces him to alter the course some, but the destination usually remains the same.

## The Magic of Written Goals

Writing down a set of goals can happen only after the hidden spark is searched out and revealed. But even then, nothing measurable can happen until the goals are written down.

No one can explain it exactly, but something almost magical happens when goals are written out. It has to do with the way God created us and is emphasized in the Scripture from Habakuk that tells us to *write the vision* and make it plain. Once we see them before our eyes on paper, the goals somehow take on a life of their own. It opens the way for ideas of plans and strategies to be developed—plans and strategies that may have lain dormant before the goals were written.

On the surface all this seems relatively simple—have a goal and write it down. If it's so simple why do less than 5% of all people establish a plan for their lives and use goals as measuring sticks to get there? Several culprits are lurking to trip us up in this area.

## No focus

Having no focus was certainly my problem for many years. I wasted time on activities that contributed little or nothing to my own personal achievements in life. With no passion, I could not stay focused for very long at a time.

Many Americans suffer from this problem. They think of many things they *could* be doing. And even a few that they perhaps *should* be doing. But none of reasons for doing them are very compelling. (As the unflappable basketball coach Pat Riley says, "There's no such thing as coulda, shoulda and woulda. If you shoulda and coulda, you woulda done it.")

So those directionless ships come home from work each day, turn on the television and settle into a state of comfortable vegetation. Their hidden sparks are buried and barely smoldering.

You may have experienced this deadening lethargy. At times one hidden spark may be fanned by an idea or word that is spoken. Perhaps it's a challenge to begin a personal fitness program, and you get all excited and buy the equipment or join a health club. But with lack of focus and commitment, with no plan of action, and if the spark is never fanned into a flame, it quickly dies out.

## Spinning Your Wheels

The other hindrance to setting goals is when a person is going off in ten different directions each day and accomplishing little or nothing. It's akin to lack of focus but can be even more frustrating. It's like a car stuck in the mud. The wheels may be spinning like mad, but that vehicle is going *nowhere*. Life can become a mad whirl of running top speed from one activity to the next, only to finally one day wake up and find you are stuck in a deep rut going nowhere fast. That can be a rude awakening. Remember that activity does not always equal progress. A person in a rocking chair is moving, but going nowhere.

## Fear of Success

While it seems strange to say, some people have a deep-seated, unrecognized fear of success. Something inside them rings a loud alarm that says, "You don't deserve this," or "You can't handle this."

Motivational speaker Les Brown tells about a time when he had founded a community organization designed to empower people in their personal lives. The program became enormously successful; so successful in fact that one day Brown woke up and panicked. He was convinced that he did not have the proper leadership skills to take the program any further. He gave the reins over to another person and walked off and left it. Success was in his hands, but his fear kept it far from him for many years.

## Fear of failure

Many people never set goals because of the fear of possible failure. They much prefer to play it safe than to take even the smallest risk. It's a good thing small children are not afflicted with this common malady. Babies would never try to walk, toddlers would never crawl up on a tricycle, and grammar school kids would never take the training wheels off their two-wheelers. In spite of tumbles, crashes, and skinned knees, they doggedly take risks over and over again.

No, we have to become all-wise, all-knowing, grown-up big people before we can learn the fear of taking risks in life. For some people it is better to never try than to try and fail. In their mind a goals list holds more threat than promise.

## To Fail Is to Quit Trying

You're never a failure at anything until you quit trying. We all know the stories of people who refused to give up.

Thomas A. Edison struggled for years to discover the correct material for the incandescent bulb (predecessor to our modern light bulb). His attempts numbered right around 10,000. Never one to be discouraged, Edison simply stated that he'd learned 10,000 ways *not* to make a light bulb.

Most everyone has heard of Macy's Department Store. But how many people know that R.H. Macy failed *seven* times before his store in New York City caught on.

Babe Ruth had many more strikeouts in his career than home runs. Did that bother him? Nope. He told his fans that every strikeout brought him closer to another home run.

Why was the Model T called the Model T? Because Ford had tried and failed with Models A through S before being successful in producing and marketing the "T."

These are the risk-takers in life—the ones who have a passion, who know how to fan the sparks of that passion, and never give up until the goal is reached.

We often think of risk-takers as fearless people. That's not true. Few people in this world are truly fearless. The difference is when you rule over the fear, rather than letting the fear rule you. Once the truths about success and failure, risk and reward, are fully understood, goal-setting and life-planning will no longer serve be a threat. Instead it will be a project that holds the promise of a better future.

## Suck-It-Up Summary

- goals that are not written are goals that are not tangible
- dreams turn into goals when a deadline is attached to it
- many hindrances can arise to stop you from setting goals; identify those hindrances and move past them
- change the *threat* of a goal into the *promise* of a goal

## Suck-It-Up Steps to Success

List hindrances that have arisen in your life that have stopped you from setting and achieving your goals.

_____

_____

_____

_____

_____

_____

List areas in which you feel that specific goal setting will help to achieve your objectives

_____

_____

_____

_____

_____

_____

66

*Anything worth doing is worth doing terrible —*
*until you learn to do it terrific.*

**– Scot Knight**

• • • • •

*You gain strength, courage, and confidence*
*by every experience in which*
*you really stop to look fear in the face . . . .*
*You must do the thing you think you cannot do.*

**– Eleanor Roosevelt**

99

# Chapter 7
# What's It Going to Cost?

## Obstacles

Once your goals are written out on paper, and when the plans and strategies to reach those goals are firmly set in your mind, then the obstacles that pop up along the way will appear much smaller and inconsequential. Circumstances that previously might have knocked you to the ground, will now only cause you to lose your balance for a short time. Why? Because your perspective has totally changed. Obstacles will look like obstacles only if you take your eyes off the goal.

## Staying Power

Where does staying power come from? Why do some people stay down after they stumble and fall? Why do others get up time after time? What is the stuff staying power is made of?

Once I was accepted into chiropractic school, once I'd moved to Dallas, taken prerequisite courses and enrolled, I came within a hair's breadth of tossing in the towel and quitting. I remember the moment vividly.

It was the third week into school. I was sitting in anatomy class trying to listen and trying hard to take a few notes. I mentioned earlier that I was never a good student, and nothing much had changed in my four years of college. I made it through, but certainly not with A's or B's. As I sat there in anatomy class, I'd never felt dumber.

The professor was talking about the anatomy of the bone, the layers of the bone, the bone marrow, the cells of the bone. He was saying words like *osteoclast* and *osteoblast*, words I couldn't even pronounce, let alone spell. Suddenly I got a sick feeling in the pit of my stomach. This just wasn't working. I remember the moment sitting there in class when I laid my pencil down on my notepad and thought, "I can't do this. I don't know who I've been trying to fool, but I'm not smart enough to become a doctor. I don't have what it takes. I'll *never* have what it takes. I'm quitting right now."

That class seemed to drag on for hours, but I had stopped listening to the lecture. All I could think of was, "How am I going to tell Mama that I'm quitting chiropractic school?"

When the class was over, an interesting thing happened. Of course no one was aware that I was experiencing a fierce inward struggle, least of all my buddy who was sitting right beside me. At the end of class he leaned over to me and said, "Hey Scot, guess what? There's a lady in this class who is real smart. She has beautiful handwriting and takes perfect notes almost word for word. She's going to make copies of her notes and share them with anyone who wants them."

## Taking Small Steps

On the surface that might have been an insignificant bit of news, but to me it was as though someone had tossed out a lifeline. Notes. I could get the notes from someone—someone who could spell the words and get them right. And I could study those notes. That offered me one small step that I could take that very day. Suddenly what had a few moments earlier seemed totally overwhelming and impossible, didn't seem so overwhelming any more. I would study the notes from that day's lecture. After the next class session, I would study the notes from that day's lecture. I would take it one step at a time, one class at a time, one day at a time. Breaking it down into small steps made it all seem much more doable.

The lesson proved to be a valuable one. From that point on, whenever I was faced with a challenge that appeared to be overwhelming, I stopped and considered how I could break it down into small doable steps. When facing the long days after I opened my first practice and no one showed up, I realized I had to take life one day at a time, one step at a time. That's all that got me through those first months.

## One Day at a Time

This is one of the basic concepts taught by Alcoholic Anonymous—to live life one day at a time, to take challenges in life one step at a time. That simple concept has saved many lives through the years including that of Los Angeles Dodger pitcher, Bob Welch. Welch, who grew up in a hard-drinking town outside of Detroit had his first drink when he was barely ten years old.

By the time he attended college, alcohol was getting the best of him, but it would be a long time before he could admit his problem. When he was drafted into the Dodgers' minor league team in 1977, he quickly learned that beer and alcohol was everywhere—and often free. Such easy access to alcohol worked to speed up his downfall.

After he was involved in an auto accident in which several of his teammates barely escaped injury, Welch was finally persuaded to seek rehabilitation.

Arriving for spring training in 1980, he announced to the entire ball club that he was an alcoholic, adding that his only hope was to stop drinking one day at a time. Welch went on to become a valuable ball player. In 1990, he won twenty-seven games for the Oakland Athletics and earned the Cy Young Award as the best pitcher in his league. And he did it all—one day at a time.

Whether it's facing a challenge such as weight loss, or getting free from a debilitating habit, it helps to break the goals down into doable steps to be completed in a measurable space of time.

What will you do this day that will move you one step closer to your goal?

## The Blame Game Is a Lame Game

I had some hard knocks while I was growing up. Mama worked very hard to support us, but there was never much money to be had. Because I hated doing schoolwork, I relied on my wit and my antics to pull me through. I was the one who was cutting up during class and causing all sorts of distractions. That was probably my way of compensating for being unable to do my class work.

It would have been super easy to use these circumstances as excuses for failure. I've found that people who accomplish very little in life usually have a string of excuses to validate the reasons for their failures or lack of achievements. It's the old *blame game* and it's certainly nothing new. Adam and Eve played that game in the Garden of Eden. The blame game is a lame game in which everyone loses and nobody wins. In order to play the blame game, there has to be a shift of responsibility.

My Mama would never let me get away with that. She had no patience with whimpering, whining, or shifting the blame. "Suck it up and step out," means taking ownership for what happens in your life. It means shouldering the responsibility of making the most of the hand that life deals you. You suck it up and do the best with what you've got. It's part of the price you pay to get what you want in life.

## Paying the Price

It certainly wasn't easy spending long hours working in the oil fields and going to school at night in order to get into college the next fall. Especially when all my friends were having so much fun playing around. Blaming the circumstances would not have made the situation any easier. By taking responsibility, and by taking action, I had no time to whine, complain, or blame.

I'm thankful I learned this lesson early. It's saved me hours of grief and despair. Especially when I faced the very difficult National tests upon graduating from Chiropractic school.

## Exerting Extra Effort

There were days during chiropractic school when I spent as much as fifteen hours studying for certain tests. Many of my buddies could get it down in about five hours, and then they were ready to party. "No," I'd tell them. "I can't go. I've got to stay right here and study." Every day, in almost every subject, I faced an uphill battle.

As I was finishing up school, I had no problem at all with Clinic. In Clinic, students had to have twelve new patients, and had to give a hundred adjustments. I whizzed through Clinic finishing as one of the top five in a class of about eighty. Taking the National Boards was something else entirely.

For the national exams there is a Part I, Part II, and Part III. (Since that time, an additional Part IV has been added.) Part I consisted of six different areas, including such things as physiology and chemistry. I flunked physiology in phase one of my National Boards. Needless to say, I was disappointed, but I just turned right around and took it again. And I flunked it a *second* time. What a perfect time to schedule a pity party.

By now it was time for graduation, and all my classmates were completing Parts II and III and I was still stuck at Part I. It was a bad situation made worse by the fact that I'd been offered an associate position by a chiropractor from Bay City, Texas. Since I had not passed the national exam I could not accept his offer. Everything on the surface looked very bleak. It was time once again to *suck it up and step out*.

I saw no sense in whining, complaining or blaming. I got to work and started investigating. I learned that there are three states that allow chiropractors to practice without completing all boards—West Virginia, Nevada and Oklahoma. It's not that their standards are lower, but their requirements are set up differently.

By this time, I'd met my beautiful wife-to-be, Tara, who just happened to be from Oklahoma. Since her hometown of Oklahoma City was only three hours from Dallas, we looked for a place near there. I settled on a small town of about 16,000 where there was only one other chiropractor.

I've told in an earlier chapter how I struggled and worked to get the practice underway and growing. During that time, I took Parts I, II, and III of the National Boards and passed all of them. Now there was a new Part IV that I would have to pass, and it would be the most difficult of all.

I learned there was a study course being offered in Dallas that lasted a week. It started at four in the afternoon and lasted until ten at night. I knew if I took that study course, I would be able to pass the national exams for Part IV.

First of all, the course wasn't cheap. I had to scrape the money together. And by now I had enough patients that I couldn't afford to close the clinic. Each day I treated patients from eight in the morning until one in the afternoon. I then drove to Dallas and attended class until ten. Drove back to Oklahoma, grabbed a few hours sleep, and did it all over again the following day. I was determined to do whatever the situation demanded to reach my goal. And the sacrifice paid off! I passed Part IV with flying colors, making a 92 on the exam. I was jumping for joy!

## Suck-It-Up Summary

- obstacles appear smaller when your eyes are on the goal
- break goals down into small manageable steps; each with its own separate deadline
- avoid playing the blame game where no one wins
- whatever it takes—do it

## Suck-It-Up Steps to Success

List ways in which you can break up your major goals into smaller, more manageable steps

_____

_____

_____

_____

_____

_____

_____

66

*Every man, however wise,*
*needs the advice of some sage friend*
*in the affairs of life.*

**– Plautus**

• • • • •

*Keep away from people who try*
*to belittle your ambitions.*
*Small people always do that,*
*but the really great make you feel*
*that you, too, can become great.*

**– Mark Twain**

# Chapter 8
# You Are Who You Run With

## God's Choices and Our Choices

There are times when God puts very special people in our lives. I can testify to that with regard to my mother. She has been my guiding star and my front row cheerleader all through my growing up years. I didn't choose her, God chose her for me.

The same way with the man who saw me fall from the balcony that day when I was only eight years old. He undoubtedly saved my life. I felt he was an angel sent from God.

But for the most part, we choose our companions, our friends, our associates. We choose the people we hang out with. If I heard Mama say this old saying once, I heard her say it a hundred times—*"Birds of a feather flock together."* I say the same thing, only I word it little differently—*You are who you run with.* In other words, you will reflect the mannerisms and thought patterns of the people with whom you are in constant contact.

Looking back over the years, I truly am thankful for the good people I chose to associate myself with. Keith Harrell in his book, *Attitude is Everything* refers to these people as his *A-Team*. I like that. They are our encouragers, they are our sounding boards. They are the people who are there when you need them. These relationships do not happen on accident. They must be cultivated like a well-watered flower garden in the midst of a scorching West Texas summer.

## High School Sweetheart

I remember growing up in a loving home, always attending church with my mother, but I really never knew anything about the concept of being saved, dunked in a tank, and having a relationship with Christ. That is, not until I began dating one particular girl my senior year of high school. She had an amazing impact on my life. Not only was she active in school, but she was also active in her church and its youth program. Because I liked her and wanted to impress her, I would skip out of attending my own church and go with her.

Eventually all that exposure to the Gospel finally took hold on me. On January 26, 1986, I accepted Christ as my Lord and Savior and became a Christian. It was a landmark day for me and changed the course of my life.

It was not in God's plan for this girl and me to be life partners, but it was in His plan for her to be instrumental in leading me to Him. As a result of her impact on my life, I married a Christian girl, and we are raising our daughter in a Christian home using Godly principles. I will be eternally grateful for that.

## Diran

My college buddy, Diran, became yet another Christian friend who helped me through a few tight places.

During Chiropractic school, I had one instructor who gave me fits. The class was Pathology, the study of diseases. I went to this instructor to ask how to study for her tests and she informed me that if I studied from her notes I would do well. Since I memorize easily, I assured myself I could do this with no problem. While other students were studying old tests that floated around the class, I spent time on the notes. However, when test time came around and I looked over the test in front of me, my confidence slipped down the tubes. I saw nothing on this test that I'd studied. Upset and miffed I later confronted the instructor, but got no satisfaction in her responses. She acted as though it'd been all my fault. I now had an F in the class. If I flunked out, it would put me six months behind in graduating, plus adding another $10,000 to my already-hefty tuition loan total.

When the next test came along, I wised up and studied all the old tests. When test time came around again—you guessed it— the test was based on all her class notes. I now had two flunked tests on my records. I was ready to give up and call it quits. I couldn't win for losing. I had no energy to even be angry; instead, I was totally discouraged, drowning in hopelessness. That's when Diran stepped up to the plate for me.

Diran, an ex-football player from Texas Tech, was the Christian in my group of friends who never drank, but liked to party. Oh, he went to the parties with us, but never to my knowledge, did he ever drink. Into my darkness of despair, he spoke life and hope through his Christian actions.

"Scot," he said to me, "now you stop worrying. We've still got one more test, and that test is worth 50% of your class grade. You're gonna pass this. You've got what it takes, and I'm gonna make sure you pass it."

Diran was as good as his word. When it came time for the final exam, this good friend came to get me. "I don't want any phones ringing, and I don't want any interruptions," Diran said. "We're gonna study, study, study." So we went out to supper, then we rented a motel room.

And study we did. I remember watching as Diran spread out all those old tests on one of the beds. Then beside them, he spread out all our class notes. And we studied first the notes, then the old tests, then the notes, and then the old tests. We studied straight through until three in the morning.

As we were finishing up, Diran said, "Scot? You mind if I say a prayer for us?" I surely didn't mind. "Please do," I answered. It was an interesting prayer that Diran prayed. Simple, yet interesting. "Dear Lord," he said, "I'm not asking specifically that Scot pass this test tomorrow, but I am asking that everything we studied tonight will be on that test!" I added my hearty, "Amen!"

And God did just that. I whizzed through the test and when the scores came back I'd made a 92. I passed the course, and I attribute it directly to the fact that I was hanging out with the right people. Diran never once agreed with me in my despair. He continually spoke words of hope and encouragement to me. I don't believe I could have ever passed that class without him being right by my side.

## Shayne Walker

After selling my practice in Oklahoma and moving to Round Rock, Texas, I learned that there was another new chiropractic clinic opening just a few doors down from where I'd located. His grand opening was schedule for July 3, 1998, and mine was to be August 3, 1998. I didn't think much about it at the time, but I made a good choice when I reached out a hand of friendship to Dr. Shayne Walker. I guess I could have viewed him as a threat, but we were both new to the town and I felt we needed one another.

I walked down to his clinic one day and introduced myself to Shayne. I learned that this was his first clinic, and since I'd already been operating a clinic for four years I gave him all the help and assistance I possibly could. He didn't have an x-ray machine, so I offered him the use of ours. When one of his patients needed an x-ray, he'd call us and then send his patient down the street and we'd shoot x-rays for him.

Shane graduated from the same Chiropractic school in Dallas just a few years behind me, so we knew many of the same instructors and shared lots of funny stories. In our downtime, while building up our clientele, we'd drive around town together, having our calls forwarded to our cell phones. Because Shayne was a single guy,

Tara and I invited him over for a home-cooked meal once or twice a week. Before you knew it, we had become best friends.

I never viewed having another chiropractor in the same neighborhood as a threat. I just felt that we both could help each other. Because of that, God has used Shayne as a sounding board for me, and a voice of encouragement all along the way.

Shayne has been an instrumental part of my stepping out and becoming a professional speaker.

## Tara (Soul Mate)

Have you ever met a woman who can out-cook Martha Stewart? Or out-perform Sheryl Swoopes? More positive than Zig Ziglar? More friendly than Will Rogers? On top of that, she could easily submit articles to parenting magazines on how to become the best mother ever. That, my friends, is my wife, Tara.

I have never in my life met a more positive, people-oriented, giving, loving, caring individual than this person whom I call my "soul mate." Tara always supports me, she encourages me, she believes in me and stands beside me in all my endeavors—I mean *all* my endeavors.

God truly blessed my life the day he placed Tara in my path. I firmly believe that we become whom we associate with, and being married to Tara has forever changed and altered my life for the better. I thank God every day for my beautiful wife.

## You Can't Play with Trash and Stay Clean

Many a teenager has gotten off track in life simply because he or she chose wrong friends and decided to run with the wrong crowd. Tim Allen of *Home Improvement* fame was just such a kid. In college he had no focus and no direction in his life. He had no idea what he wanted to do. Due to the sudden death of his father when Tim was only eleven, his heart and mind became filled with bitterness.

While he was a relatively bright student making good grades at Western Michigan University in Kalamazoo, Tim fell in with the party crowd. His life soon consisted of non-stop parties where drugs were in easy possession. He impressed his professors with his humor, his wit, and his writing abilities, but that wasn't strong enough to pull him away from the negative influence of the wrong crowd. After graduating in 1976, he made his living selling drugs for almost two full years. On October 2, 1978, Tim was arrested for selling cocaine.

The arrest shocked him, as did the sixty horrifying days in a holding cell before his arraignment. Once out on bail, Tim took a new look at his life and realized that all he'd ever really wanted to do was be a comedian. Although he made positive steps in that direction during the next few months, it was too late to stop the inevitable. The judge handed him a five-year sentence of which he served eighteen months.

Thankfully, Allen used his prison term to perfect his comedy routine and put it to good use upon his release. He learned from his mistakes and went on to make great strides in the world of television and motion picture comedy. But first he had to learn a very hard lesson about choice of friends.

## Choose Spark-Igniters

Stop and think a moment about the people you spend time with on a daily basis. What do you hear them say? Do they ignite your sparks? Or do they constantly speak negative comments, dousing your sparks? Do they see the worst of every situation? Do they try to talk you out of your dreams? Do you hear them telling you that your plans will never work? Or that you will never accomplish what you have set out to do?

It may be time to stop and think about where you're going in life, and what it will take to get you there. If all your friends and associates are mediocre thinkers, you will have difficult choices to make. Perhaps it's time to seek out new friends.

Those who douse your inner sparks are the ones you should be wary of. No need to be rude or unkind to them, but realize that they cannot see your dreams. In fact, your dreams and visions may frighten them, or in some cases, threaten them. Don't take it personally. They are only saying what they think and believe—it just doesn't happen to be what you think and believe!

Look for a mentor who will be your spark-igniter. Do you know someone who lives his or her life as you would like to live yours? Call that person and make a connection. If you have no one personally, then think about finding a mentor through motivational books and tapes.

Right now, as you are reading *Suck it Up and Step Out*, allow me to be your coach, your encourager, your spark-igniter. It is vital that you have someone in your corner cheering you on. Going at it alone is not impossible, but it's certainly more difficult.

## Suck-It-Up Summary
- choose close friends carefully; look for those who help ignite your sparks
- weed negative people out of your life by allowing them less and less of your quality time and attention
- seek out a mentor who can coach you, encourage you, and lead you

## Suck-It-Up Steps to Success
Make a list of the people you associate with on a daily basis. List them all—friends, family members, associates, co-workers, church friends. Sort the list to find your spark-igniters and try to spend quality time with those individuals.

------------------------------------------

------------------------------------------

------------------------------------------

"

*No one can make me feel
inferior but myself.*

**– Eleanor Roosevelt**

• • • • •

*The more you like yourself,
the less you are like anyone else,
which makes you unique.*

**– Walt Disney**

"

# Chapter 9
# Be Your Own Spark-Igniter

## Positive Self-Talk

O nly you have the choice to choose to change. And one of the areas where any person can make major changes is in our inner thoughts—that voice we hear speaking inside our heads. In a world that capitalizes on bad news in every segment of the media, learning to speak positively is a must! Many people are not aware that the cells of the body respond directly to our thoughts and attitudes. That's why the Bible tells us that "a merry heart does good like a medicine." (Proverbs 17:22) Positive affirmations work to keep our bodies and minds in good health.

## Minor in the Weaknesses; Major in the Strengths

In order to suck it up and step out, you need to know who you are. Learn to recognize your own strengths and weaknesses. Many people waste time fretting over weaknesses, when they could be spending that valuable time building up their strengths.

I knew early on that I was not the best student in the world, and that I would have to study longer and harder than most of my friends. I could have thrown up my hands and said, "I'm just not college material. I'll get a menial job and try to make the best of a bad situation." Studying may have been my weakness, but tenacity is definitely one of my strengths. I'm a pretty determined person. I simply allowed the latter to carry the former and I made it!

While I may not be as "book smart" as others, I'm definitely a people person. My personality is such that I'm not afraid to walk up to a total stranger and shake hands and start a friendly conversation. I recognize that personal strength in myself and use it to good advantage whenever possible. If I were not so out-going, I might not have taken that step to get out and meet my business neighbors, an act which essentially allowed me to save my first chiropractic clinic.

I know many people who are well versed in their weaknesses and prove it by talking about them every day. Their strengths, they're not so sure about. God has given to each of us our own unique personality. It is vitally important for each person to understand his or her own personality and cooperate with that personality.

## Only You Can Create Your Limitations

What's Stopping You? On a day-to-day basis, what stops you from doing what it takes to fulfill your dreams? What stops you from sucking it up and stepping out?

Below is a list of self-imposed limitations people put on themselves, whether real or imagined. Obviously this is not a complete list, but these are certainly the major ones. Do any of these belong to you?

- Blame
- Fear
- Feelings of inferiority
- Lack of parental or family support
- Lack of economic advantage

## Blame

We touched on blame in Chapter 7 as an obstacle that can rise up to keep us from achieving our goals. It is definitely a self-imposed limitation. Blaming circumstances or other people is a real cop out in life. It wastes precious hours of time, and accomplishes nothing.

Mountain climber Erik Weihenmayer has conquered some of the greatest heights on the planet, such as Mt. Rainier in Washington State, Long's Peak in Colorado, Mt. Kilimanjaro in Tanzania, and Mt. McKinley in Alaska. While there have been scores of mountain climbers who have done that and more, the amazing things about Erik is that he is blind!

Erik began losing his sight as a young boy, but it never stopped him from playing sports and riding his bicycle. By the time he was in high school, his sight was totally gone. Just as Erik was learning to adjust to a sightless world, his mother was killed in a tragic car wreck. Although those days were extremely difficult, he never allowed any adverse circumstances in his life to become excuses. In Erik's life he had no time for blame. In addition to his mountain climbing adventures, Erik completed college and became an elementary school teacher.

When you're tempted to play the blame game, think of people like Erik who could have easily blamed his circumstances, but chose not to.

## Fear

When opportunities come knocking on your door, do you fail to answer because of fear? If so, you're not alone. Fear is a debilitating emotion, which is also highly contagious. And it can easily attach itself to those who are unaware and unsuspecting. Fear can slow you down and keep you from reaching the dreams and goals you have in life. How can one emotion be so powerful? Because fear is sneaky. A good way to think of fear is with this acronym:

**F**alse

**E**vidence

**A**ppearing

**R**eal

Fear tells you things are real when indeed they are false. When we believe our fears, when we give in to our fears, we are virtually paralyzed.

There is, of course, a healthy fear. There's the fear that makes you run from a snake that slithers out from the flower bushes in your back yard. Healthy fear restrains you from walking down the middle of the highway when a diesel truck is bearing down. Healthy fear leads us to use wisdom in many areas of our lives. David Ben-Gurion said it this way, "Courage is a special kind of knowledge: the knowledge of how to fear what ought to be feared and how not to fear what ought not to be feared."

Unhealthy, unnatural fear is much different than healthy fear, and the unhealthy fear is the kind I'm addressing now. Fears that are not recognized, confronted, and overcome can plague a person for years and years. They need to be recognized for what they are.

It's a common misconception that highly successful people are never afraid. That they just plow through life like so many Green Bay Packers linebackers, bowling over obstacles as they go. The truth is, successful people have just as many fears as anyone else. The only difference is how the fears are handled. Successful people identify fears, face fears, then move forward *in spite of the fears*! There's the secret! They control the fears rather than allowing fears to control them.

You may have a dream in your heart, and a goal in your mind, but you're afraid of what might happen if you fail. Fear of failure is nothing new to me. I experienced it all through college and all through chiropractic school. That's why December, 1993, was such an important time in my life—my graduation from chiropractic school. I had faced my fears, tackled them fully and wrestled them to the ground. I came forth as the victor! No one can ever take that joy and sense of accomplishment from me. I've seen people who were much smarter than me throw in the towel and quit, or worse yet, never even try due to fears. Fears they refused to face, or even identify. What a waste of potential!

When actor Jack Lemmon snagged the lead part in *Days of Wine and Roses* in the early 1960s, he admitted to being scared to death. Why? Because up until then, he'd played only comedy roles. Now he was stepping into an area that was, at that time, completely out of his comfort zone. Although he knew it was a good part, he was terrified he'd not be able to play it well. Rather than allow the fear to debilitate him, he used the fear to propel him to do his very best. He sucked it up and stepped out. As a result, Lemmon received an Academy Award nomination that year as best actor.

## Feelings of Inferiority

Almost every person alive can cite reasons for experiencing feelings of inferiority—some may even seem valid. Because of that, inferiority becomes one of the more common self-imposed limitations.

The late Katharine Meyer Graham, owner of the *Washington Post*, was born—as they say—with a silver spoon in her mouth. Her father's copper mining industry had made him a multi-millionaire. But in the shadow of her talented older siblings and her famous and inattentive parents, Katharine felt like a "plodding peasant," as she put it. When she invited girlfriends over to spend the night, the servants who set breakfast before them were a source of embarrassment to little Kay Meyer. All she ever longed for was a normal home with loving parents.

As an adult, even though Katharine was worth millions, she had no concept of how to handle money and by her own confession did not even know what a mortgage was. Upon her marriage, she found she was totally ignorant of how to keep house and rear children. Her ignorance of even the most basic of life skills created a great sense of low self-esteem within Katharine.

No matter how intense those feelings were, she was determined not to allow the inferiority to stop her. She set out to educate herself in many areas. When her husband Phil Graham committed suicide in 1963, Katharine boldly stepped forward and took the reins of the *Post*. Under her steady leadership, the newspaper grew to become one of the best and most powerful in the nation.

All through her life, Katharine Graham never lost her zeal to learn—but she always felt she was pressed to hurry to make up for lost time.

Because of my difficulties as a student in grade school, I too struggled with feelings of inferiority. This is probably the reason I became the clown, hiding my feelings of lack behind the mask of crazy-acting. One day I had to face the fact that I was the only person who could change those feelings. Like Katharine Graham, I made the choice not to let inferiority pull me down or defeat me. Only *you* can make the choice to choose to change. It's up to you. It's up to me.

Famous guitarist Chet Atkins admits that feelings of inferiority dogged him nearly all his life. Shyness prevented him from speaking to people, but he could play his guitar for them. Atkins made sure his desire to become a famous guitar player won out over the feelings of inferiority.

## Lack of Parental or Family Support

I count myself truly fortunate and blessed to have grown up with a mother who encouraged me on a daily basis. I've wondered at times what kind of person I might be today had I not had her undying support. Might I have used that as an excuse not to rise to my highest potential? Possibly. But I like to think not. I like to think I might have been like the boy named Paul who grew up in Arkansas during the depression.

Paul was a big kid, bigger than the other guys in his school. Paul came from a poor family, but one with dignity and high morals. By the time he was in the eighth grade, Paul would linger after school and watch his school football team practice. There was a longing in his heart to be out on that field. Two things prevented him from doing so. First of all, football season came about when he was needed in the cotton fields to help get in the cotton crop. And secondly, his parents felt that football was a "worldly" sport and therefore they would not allow him to play.

One day while Paul watched the team from his spot behind the school building, the football coach happened to see him there. Noting his mammoth size, the coach invited the student to enter into the practice. The boy joined in with amazing grit and gusto. His excitement knew no bounds. Eventually, his mother convinced his father to allow Paul to join the team and play the game of football.

Paul played with the same intensity throughout every game, even when he was hurt. Third quarter, fourth quarter. Didn't matter. He played full-speed every second he was on the field. All through his high school years of playing the game his parents never attended one of his games. Not one. But Paul never let that stop him. Nor did he see it as an excuse.

From high school, the Arkansas plowboy attended Alabama University on a football scholarship and played football for all four years of college. Again, his parents never attended a game, nor did they ever give their approval or blessing.

Because the university did not want to lose a young man who had such passions and love for the game of football, they offered the young 23-year-old graduate a spot on their staff as coach. Paul "Bear" Bryant lived and breathed football all his adult life, winning the respect and admiration of the entire national football community for being a diligent, fair, conservative coach. Bear Bryant became a legend in the game of football.

It never occurred to him to allow his parents' obvious lack of support to be used as an obstacle or excuse. "If you believe in yourself and have pride and never quit, you'll be a winner," he said. "The price of victory is high but so are the rewards." He took his own advice to heart.

Not everyone is fortunate enough to have a set of parents who are supportive and encouraging. But as Bear Bryant so eloquently proved, that one lack doesn't have to be an obstacle or hindrance to fulfilling your personal dreams.

## Lack of Economic Advantage

"If I could only win the lottery." "If I could only win the Clearing House Sweepstakes." "If I could only inherit the fortune of some rich relative."

Ever hear people make remarks like these? Perhaps you have said them yourself. What is perceived as a lack of economic advantage holds many people back from achieving their dreams. In their minds, lack of finances is the biggest obstacle in their roadway to success.

When I made the decision to go to college, I had no resources to do so. Mama and I had not been saving our pennies in order to make that happen. (In our home, there were never any extra pennies *to* save.) How easy it would have been to blame my inability to attend college on the fact that we had no money. I chose not to do that. How thankful I am today that I made that decision.

A little boy name Sammy grew up incredibly poor in the country of the Dominican Republic. A lover of baseball, the little boy made his first ball glove out of an inside-out milk carton. His bat was a branch from a vasima tree that grew in his neighborhood. He and his friends fashioned a ball from an old golf ball, around which they wrapped torn, discarded nylon stockings, then covered the whole thing with black tape. With these meager bits of sports equipment, the Sammy and his friends played ball with all their hearts.

When Sammy came to the States to play baseball as a teenager, he could not speak English, he was physically malnourished, and he lacked the formal coaching that most of his American teammates had enjoyed. But Sammy Sosa never let those circumstances stop him or even slow him down. He had to work harder than anyone else on the team, but that was all right with him. This determined baseball player, who never let his economic standing hold him back, went on to re-write baseball history.

## Suck-It-Up Summary

- you and only you create self-imposed limitations of blame, fear, feelings of inferiority and lack of economic advantage

- be your own cheerleader by using positive thoughts and affirmations; ignite your own sparks

- only you can choose to change your own thoughts, words, and actions

## Suck-It-Up Steps to Success

If you have been blaming people or circumstances for your own lack of success, list those here. Give the list a close look. No one ever wins the blame game. Suck it up and step out!

_____

_____

_____

_____

_____

_____

Next do the same thing with the unspoken (or spoken) fears. Make a list of fears that are holding you back. Are you afraid of failing? Are you afraid of success? Are you afraid of what your friends and family will say if you strike out and begin to achieve your dreams? See the fears for what they really are: False Evidence Appearing Real.

_____

_____

_____

_____

_____

What things have happened in your life that may have made you feel inferior to others? Make a list. As you write out the list, new thoughts may surface that never occurred to you before. What makes you feel "less than" some other person? Realize those feelings are not going to disappear automatically. But identifying them will help you understand and deal with your reactions. It's time to stop allowing those *feelings* of inferiority to prevent you from achieving your dreams and goals. Whatever has happened in the past is just that—past! Time to move on. Time to suck it up and step out.

_____

_____

_____

_____

_____

You may have grown up in a family that offered no encouragement or support, whether it be parents or siblings. If that has been true in your life—even today in your adult life—ask yourself if you are still using that as an excuse. List the ways in which you have allowed the lack of family support to stop you or slow you down.

_____

_____

_____

_____

Lack of money or economic advantages can be an obstacle in your life *only if you allow it to be.* The story of Sammy Sosa is only one of hundreds that could be cited of people who have started out with very little cash on hand, and yet accomplished great, often amazing, things. Make a list of areas in which you have felt lack of money has stopped you or slowed you down in your goals.

_____

_____

_____

_____

_____

Now make a list of steps you *can take* toward your goals in spite of the fact that money is in short supply. Once you begin to brainstorm, your creativity will come into play and you will see possibilities pop up that might never have occurred to you before. Robert Schuller likes to call this "possibility thinking." By now you know what *I* call it—"Suck it up and step out!" Step out and make your list today. Don't wait!

_____

_____

_____

_____

_____

_____

You can't really begin moving forward to achieve your dreams and reach your goals until these obstacles are out of the way—or at least minimized.

**"**

*Many people have climbed*
*to the top rung of the ladder*
*of what they thought was "success"*
*only to find out that it was*
*leaning against the wrong wall.*

**"**

# Chapter 10
# Wanting What You Get Is as Important as Getting What You Want

When you begin striving toward a definite goal, be very sure you wind up where you want to be when you attain that goal. Sound confusing? Let me explain.

When I headed for Oklahoma and set up my practice, I couldn't think any further than wanting to have a successful practice. I would have a decent income; I would be accepted in the community; I would be helping people. I thought that was the *end-all* dream of my lifetime. I was shocked and a little saddened to find out that it was not! At least not in the place where I was.

## Stuck in the Rut

After a few years, we were earning in excess of $25,000 a month. The practice was thriving and I had more patients than I could handle. We were active in the community. We had two nice vehicles. We bought a beautiful home, fixed it up, and decorated it just like we wanted. We saw it added to the town's Christmas Tour of Homes two years in a row. On the surface my life seemed to be everything I'd ever wanted, but underneath something was terribly wrong.

Each morning I barely dragged out of bed by 8:15 to be at the clinic by nine, skipping breakfast. At noon I sought out an all-you-can-eat buffet and stuffed myself, then felt low and out of sorts all afternoon. Before I knew it, I'd ballooned up to 245 pounds and I was miserable. It was crazy.

The frightening thing is that I could have gone on like that for years. I know people who have. They get caught in a rut—a rut that causes them misery and grief, but they seem helpless to get out.

But my point here is not about the rut, it's about *wanting what you get*. Be sure when you *get* what you want; that you *want* what you get.

One day my wife and I had a long talk. It was no secret to her that I was not happy. After getting to the bottom of the matter, I admitted to her that while I loved my work, I wasn't happy with my surroundings.

"What do you want to do," she asked, "move to Oklahoma City?"

That was the nearest city of any size to where we lived. Her father had a chiropractic clinic there and she had many friends and relatives there.

"No," I told her. "I want to go home to Texas."

My wonderful wife simply said, "Fine then. Let's go." Just like that!

A successful business, nice home, established identity in the community—and we just walk away? If that's what it takes to move on in life, that's exactly what you have to do!

## The Floodgates Open

The moment we agreed and set our minds on our new course of action, it was as though we had opened the floodgates for things to be set in motion. First of all, I had no idea how to sell a successful chiropractic practice. (I'd only just recently learned how to set one up and run it!) Secondly, we had to figure out where we were going to move to.

I had it in my mind that I would like to live near the Austin area. I'd always liked that part of Texas, so I called the Austin Chamber of Commerce and asked to receive a package of information about the entire area.

Meanwhile I figured I would put the ad about my clinic in chiropractic magazines and up on websites to find a buyer. But before I had a chance to do that I received a phone call. The voice on the other end said, "Hello, my name is Jeff Purdle and I'm a chiropractor from Chickasha, Oklahoma. I understand your practice is for sale."

I couldn't believe it. I had only told a few of my friends and had never advertised. Jeff went on to say that his father played on a softball team in Dallas. On that team was a chiropractor who happened to mention that Scot Knight had a practice for sale near Oklahoma City. Jeff's father called him, and he turned around and called me. Six month later, he had purchased my practice for *$150,000* and Tara and I were headed for Round Rock, Texas.

## Want What You Get

It's important to take the steps to get what you want, but I have found it's equally as important to want what you actually get. Daily we read in the news of media stars and sports heroes who strived hard to get to the top. When they reached the pinnacle, to their dismay they found they were unable to handle either the fame or the riches that came with it.

Humorist and satirist, Art Buchwald grew up in foster homes during the depression. The Pulitzer Prize winner was often told by his elders that he would amount to nothing and would turn out to be no good. It was a difficult childhood by any standards.

By the time Buchwald reached the age of fifty, his success had brought him fame and fortune, and more honorary degrees than he could count. On the inside, however, he still heard the voices from when he was a kid telling him he was no good.

His wealth embarrassed him and searching for a way out he turned suicidal. It wasn't until he had spent a year and a half in therapy that he realized the voices of his childhood were wrong. Only then was he able to come to grips with the trappings that success brought with it.

Motivational speaker Les Brown often speaks about the failure of people to *prepare* for success while they are *striving* for success. Success comes and for the person who is not prepared, it can bring more misery than joy.

I'm thankful that I was able to see the rut I was in and get out. I'm also thankful for a wife who was not afraid to pull up stakes and follow me wherever I felt I needed to go. The move was a good one—a right one. And it came just in time.

## Suck-It-Up Summary

- before you get what you want be sure you want what you get; if it's not, change courses quickly
- never strive for success without preparing for success

## Suck-It-Up Steps to Success

Review the previous lists you have made in previous **Suck-It-Up Steps to Success.** Study them closely. Envision them coming to pass. Make a list of ways you can at this time prepare for the success that is coming your way.

_____

_____

_____

_____

_____

_____

# Conclusion

When I opened my first clinic and was a "for real" chiropractor, I remember a friend from school called and asked how many patients I was seeing that day. I said, "Fifty." "No way!" came back the quick retort. "You're treating fifty patients in one single day?" "No," I replied, "I'm treating twenty, but I'm SEEING fifty."

Before long the numbers began to match what I had been seeing with my mind's eye. I have learned that *it's not your eyesight that determines your future—it's your vision.*

It's my prayer that after reading this book, you too will have an expanded vision. That you will grow in your ability to see far beyond your present circumstances.

I know of no person who is born a superhuman or a saint. Those who achieve greatness in this life—as we mortals measure greatness—live in the midst in the nitty gritty grind of daily life just like you and I do. Most are average individuals who have experienced the awakening of an undeniable WANT in life. They are average individuals who have sucked it up and stepped out.

It's also my prayer that reading this book will help you to personally identify and acknowledge your undeniable WANTs. Once acknowledged, the WANTs will grow bigger and stronger. Allow yourself to envision the end result, seeing it with your mind's eye.

Set your course, using time-bound strategies that include written goals. Any goal that appears to be overwhelming should be broken down into smaller, more doable steps.

Don't listen to people who tell you it can't be done. Never take "no" for an answer. Realize there is a price to pay to reach the goal. Obstacles will arise that could stop you or slow you down. When the WANT is strong, and the course is clearly set, the obstacles will appear smaller and more insignificant.

Choose your friends and companions carefully. Seek out a mentor who has qualities you admire. Learn from that person.

Identify and squarely face the self-limiting obstacles you may have allowed to rule your life in times past.

You have skills and abilities that may now be untapped and unrealized. You have dreams that are destined to become realized goals. You have a hidden spark that *will* connect your internal drive. But how will you ever know—unless you do what my mama said to do:

## *Suck it up and step out!*